THIS
Dear Santa
Activity Book Belongs to...

_____

How To Use This Dear Santa Letters Activity Book:

This ultimate Letters to Santa notebook is a perfect way to track and record all your Dear Santa Letter memories. This unique letter to Santa activity notebook is a great way to keep all of your keepsake information all in one place.

Each interior page includes prompts and space to record the following:

1. Dear Santa My Name is - Fill In Name.

2. I Have Been - Nice, naughty or a bit of both. Choose one.

3. My Christmas Wish List - Construct your wish list using these journal lines... so as to be reminded later...

4. I Spy - Count how many Santas, Reindeer and presents then fill in how many were found.

5. Christmas Word Find - Stay on task by finding the words...cookies, sleigh, santa and circle the ones you find.

6. Christmas Ten Frames Math - to make learning more fun. And much more!

If you have kids at home for christmas, this Dear Santa Letters Activity Book is a must have! Can make an awesome gift for the holidays, and will be a keepsake memory forever.

Have Fun!

Dear Santa:

My Name is: ....

I am .... years old

I have been:
- ☐ Nice
- ☐ a lil bit naughty...but I can explain
- ☐ a bit of both

My Christmas Wish List: ....

_____

_____

_____

_____

_____

Thank you,
You are The Best Santa Ever!

Dear Santa:

My Name is:..........................

I am........... Years old

I have been:
- ☐ Nice
- ☐ a Lil bit naughty...but I can explain
- ☐ a bit of both

My Christmas Wish List:..................

_____

_____

_____

_____

Thank You,
You are The Best Santa Ever!

Dear Santa:

My Name is:..........................

I am.............. years old

I have been:
- ☐ Nice
- ☐ a lil bit naughty...but I can explain
- ☐ a bit of both

My Christmas Wish List:..................

_____
_____
_____
_____

Thank you,
You are The Best Santa Ever!

Dear Santa:

My Name is:..............................

I am........ years old

I have been:
- ☐ Nice
- ☐ a lil bit naughty...but I can explain
- ☐ a bit of both

My Christmas Wish List:..................

Thank you,
You are The Best Santa Ever!

Dear Santa:

My Name is:..............................

I am............ Years old

I have been: ☐ Nice

☐ a lil bit naughty...but I can explain

☐ a bit of both

My christmas Wish List:..................

Thank you,
You are The Best Santa Ever!

Dear Santa:

My Name is:......................

I am.............years old

I have been:
- ☐ Nice
- ☐ a lil bit naughty...but I can explain
- ☐ a bit of both

My Christmas Wish List:..................

Thank You,
You are The Best Santa Ever!

Dear Santa:

My Name is: ....

I am .... years old

I have been:
- ☐ Nice
- ☐ a lil bit naughty...but I can explain
- ☐ a bit of both

My Christmas Wish List: ....

Thank you,
You are The Best Santa Ever!

Dear Santa:

My Name is: ....

I am .... Years old

I have been:
- ☐ Nice
- ☐ a lil bit naughty...but I can explain
- ☐ a bit of both

My Christmas Wish List: ....

Thank You,
You are The Best Santa Ever!

Dear Santa:

My Name is:..............................

I am............ Years old

I have been: ☐ Nice

☐ a Lil bit naughty...but I can explain

☐ a bit of both

My Christmas Wish List:..................

Thank You,
You are The Best Santa Ever!

Dear Santa:

My name is: ....

I am .... years old

I have been:
- ☐ Nice
- ☐ a lil bit naughty...but I can explain
- ☐ a bit of both

My christmas wish list: ....

Thank you,
You are the Best Santa Ever!

Dear Santa:

My Name is: ....

I am .... years old

I have been:
- ☐ Nice
- ☐ a lil bit naughty...but I can explain
- ☐ a bit of both

My Christmas Wish List: ....

_____

_____

_____

_____

Thank you,
You are The Best Santa Ever!

Dear Santa:

My Name is: ....

I am .... Years old

I have been:
- ☐ Nice
- ☐ a Lil bit naughty...but I can explain
- ☐ a bit of both

My Christmas Wish List: ....

_____

_____

_____

_____

Thank You,
You are The Best Santa Ever!

Dear Santa:

My Name is:..........................

I am.............Years old

I have been:
- ☐ Nice
- ☐ a Lil bit naughty...but I can explain
- ☐ a bit of both

My Christmas Wish List:..................

_____

_____

_____

_____

Thank You,
You are The Best Santa Ever!

Dear Santa:

My Name is:........................

I am............ Years old

I have been:
- ☐ Nice
- ☐ a lil bit naughty...but I can explain
- ☐ a bit of both

My Christmas Wish List:................

Thank you,
You are The Best Santa Ever!

Dear Santa:

My Name is: ....

I am .... years old

I have been: ☐ Nice

☐ a lil bit naughty...but I can explain

☐ a bit of both

My Christmas Wish List: ....

Thank You,
You are The Best Santa Ever!

Dear Santa:

My Name is: ....

I am .... years old

I have been: ☐ Nice

☐ a lil bit naughty...but I can explain

☐ a bit of both

My Christmas Wish List: ....

Thank you,
You are The Best Santa Ever!

Dear Santa:

My Name is:....................

I am........ Years old

I have been: ☐ Nice

☐ a lil bit naughty...but I can explain

☐ a bit of both

My Christmas Wish List:................

_____

_____

_____

_____

Thank You,
You are The Best Santa Ever!

Dear Santa:

My name is: ....

I am .... years old

I have been:
- ☐ Nice
- ☐ a lil bit naughty...but I can explain
- ☐ a bit of both

My Christmas Wish List: ....

Thank you,
You are the Best Santa Ever!

Dear Santa:

My Name is:..........................

I am.............Years old

I have been: ☐ Nice

☐ a Lil bit naughty...but I can explain

☐ a bit of both

My Christmas Wish List:..................

_____

_____

_____

Thank You,
You are The Best Santa Ever!

Dear Santa:

My Name is:........................

I am............ Years old

I have been: ☐ Nice

☐ a Lil bit naughty...but I can explain

☐ a bit of both

My Christmas Wish List:..................

_____
_____
_____
_____

Thank You,
You are The Best Santa Ever!

Dear Santa:

My Name is:..........................

I am.............Years old

I have been: ☐ Nice

☐ a Lil bit naughty...but I can explain

☐ a bit of both

My Christmas Wish List:..................

_____

_____

_____

_____

Thank You,
You are The Best Santa Ever!

Dear Santa:

My Name is:..............................

I am............. years old

I have been:
- ☐ Nice
- ☐ a lil bit naughty...but I can explain
- ☐ a bit of both

My Christmas Wish List:..................

_____
_____
_____
_____

Thank you,
You are The Best Santa Ever!

Dear Santa:

My name is: ....

I am .... years old

I have been:

☐ Nice

☐ a lil bit naughty...but I can explain

☐ a bit of both

My Christmas Wish List: ....

_____

_____

_____

_____

Thank you,
You are the Best Santa Ever!

Dear Santa:

My Name is: ....

I am .... years old

I have been:
- ☐ Nice
- ☐ a lil bit naughty...but I can explain
- ☐ a bit of both

My Christmas Wish List: ....

_____
_____
_____
_____

Thank You,
You are The Best Santa Ever!

Dear Santa:

My name is: ....

I am .... years old

I have been:
- ☐ Nice
- ☐ a lil bit naughty...but I can explain
- ☐ a bit of both

My Christmas Wish List: ....

_____

_____

_____

_____

Thank you,
You are The Best Santa Ever!

Dear Santa:

My name is: ....

I am .... years old

I have been:
- ☐ Nice
- ☐ a lil bit naughty...but I can explain
- ☐ a bit of both

My Christmas Wish List: ....

Thank you,
You are the Best Santa Ever!

Dear Santa:

My name is: ....

I am .... years old

I have been:

☐ Nice

☐ a lil bit naughty...but I can explain

☐ a bit of both

My Christmas Wish List: ....

Thank you,
You are the Best Santa Ever!

Dear Santa:

My Name is:..............................

I am............ years old

I have been:
- ☐ Nice
- ☐ a lil bit naughty...but I can explain
- ☐ a bit of both

My Christmas Wish List:..................

_____
_____
_____
_____

Thank you,
You are The Best Santa Ever!

Dear Santa:

My Name is: ....

I am .... Years old

I have been:
- ☐ Nice
- ☐ a lil bit naughty...but I can explain
- ☐ a bit of both

My Christmas Wish List: ....

_____

_____

_____

_____

Thank you,
You are The Best Santa Ever!

Dear Santa:

My Name is:........................

I am............ Years old

I have been:
- ☐ Nice
- ☐ a Lil bit naughty...but I can explain
- ☐ a bit of both

My Christmas Wish List:..................

_____

_____

_____

_____

Thank You,
You are The Best Santa Ever!

Dear Santa:

My Name is:⁑⁑⁑⁑⁑⁑⁑⁑⁑⁑⁑⁑⁑⁑⁑⁑⁑⁑⁑⁑

I am............ Years old

I have been:
- ☐ Nice
- ☐ a Lil bit naughty...but I can explain
- ☐ a bit of both

My Christmas Wish List:..................

Thank You,
You are The Best Santa Ever!

Dear Santa:

My Name is: ....

I am .... Years old

I have been:
- ☐ Nice
- ☐ a Lil bit naughty...but I can explain
- ☐ a bit of both

My christmas Wish List: ....

_____

_____

_____

_____

Thank You,
You are The Best Santa Ever!

Dear Santa:

My Name is: ....

I am .... Years old

I have been:
- ☐ Nice
- ☐ a lil bit naughty...but I can explain
- ☐ a bit of both

My Christmas Wish List: ....

_____
_____
_____
_____

Thank You,
You are The Best Santa Ever!

Dear Santa:

My Name is:..........................

I am............ years old

I have been:
- ☐ Nice
- ☐ a Lil bit Naughty...but I can explain
- ☐ a bit of both

My christmas Wish List:..................

_____
_____
_____
_____

Thank you,
You are The Best Santa Ever!

Dear Santa:

My name is: ....

I am .... years old

I have been:
- ☐ Nice
- ☐ a lil bit naughty...but I can explain
- ☐ a bit of both

My Christmas Wish List: ....

_____
_____
_____
_____

Thank you,
You are the Best Santa Ever!

Dear Santa:

My Name is: ....

I am .... Years old

I have been:

☐ Nice

☐ a lil bit naughty...but I can explain

☐ a bit of both

My Christmas Wish List: ....

Thank You,
You are The Best Santa Ever!

Dear Santa:

My Name is: ....

I am .... years old

I have been:
- ☐ Nice
- ☐ a lil bit naughty...but I can explain
- ☐ a bit of both

My Christmas Wish List: ....

_____

_____

_____

_____

Thank You,
You are The Best Santa Ever!

Dear Santa:

My Name is: ....

I am .... years old

I have been:
- ☐ Nice
- ☐ a lil bit naughty...but I can explain
- ☐ a bit of both

My Christmas Wish List: ....

_____

_____

_____

_____

Thank You,
You are The Best Santa Ever!

CHRISTMAS WORD FIND

```
H V A I B S A N T A D C
T P S Y J W P Q Y C W R
U R D O W Z D K O V D D
C A P J G N X T R E E Z
G V D P S B V C G S Q J
N J I M G W G O T L T W
I X E P U X V O I E X R
U T U I V U W K J I Z B
H G S T O C K I N G U V
G U L S G T F E W H K E
I R E I N D E E R B X Q
P R E S E N T Z U F B N
```

WORDS TO FIND

COOKIE SLEIGH REINDEER
PRESENT STOCKING SANTA
TREE

SNOWFLAKES TEN FRAMES

NAME: _____

COLOR THE TEN FRAMES TO MATCH THE NUMBERS ON THE PICTURE

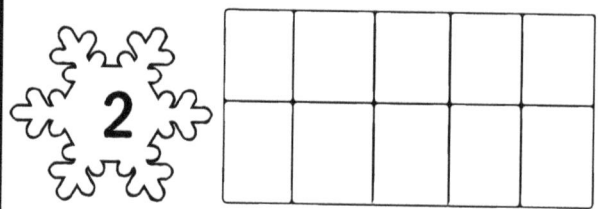

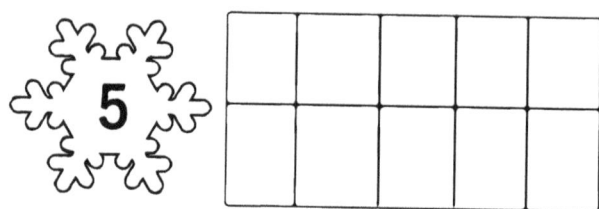

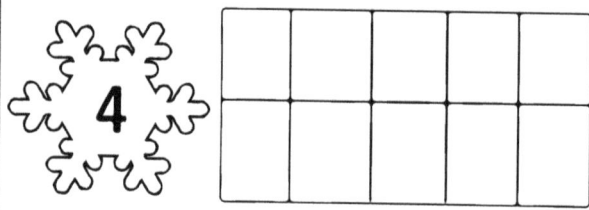

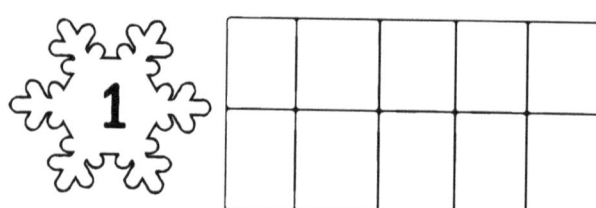

CHRISTMAS TEN FRAMES

NAME: _____

COLOR THE TEN FRAMES TO MATCH THE NUMBERS ON THE PIC

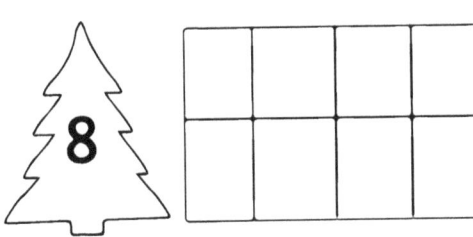
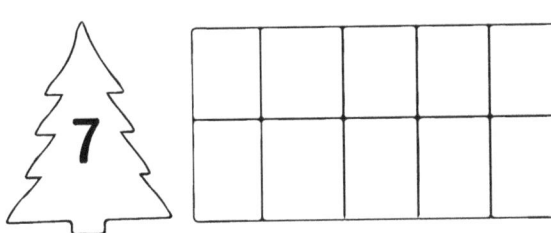
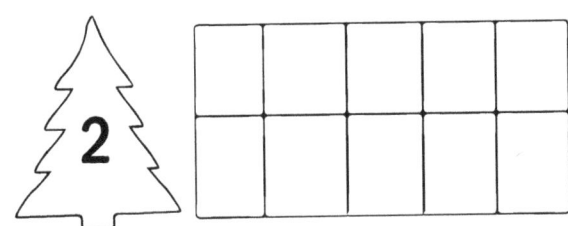
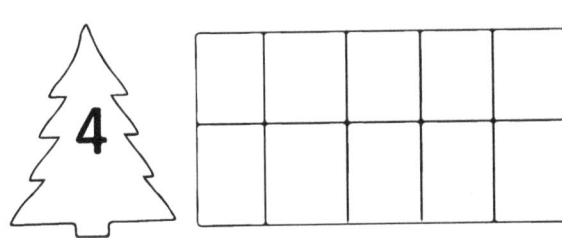
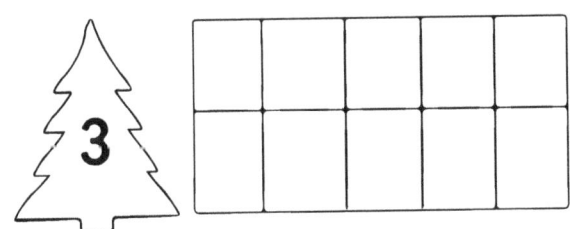
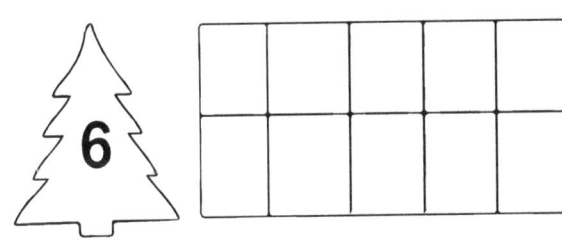
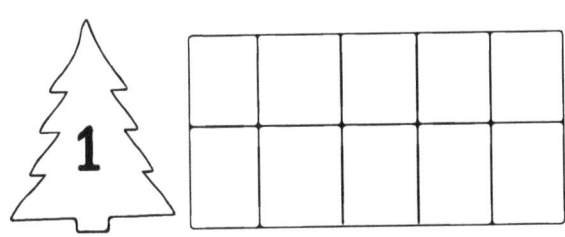

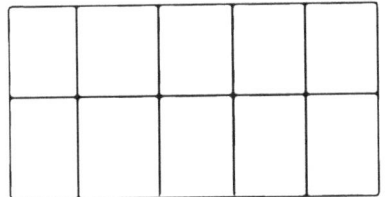

CHRISTMAS TEN FRAMES

NAME: _____

COLOR THE TEN FRAMES TO MATCH THE NUMBERS ON THE PIC

5

4

9

2

1

7

10

8

CHRISTMAS TEN FRAMES

NAME: _____

COLOR THE TEN FRAMES TO MATCH THE NUMBERS ON THE PIC

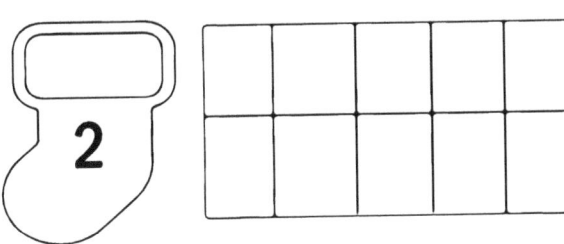
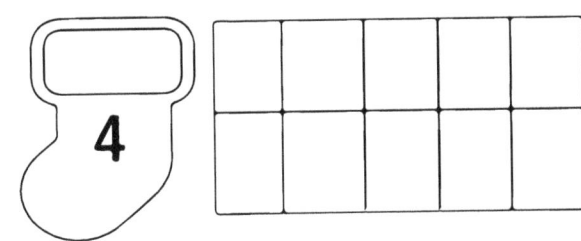
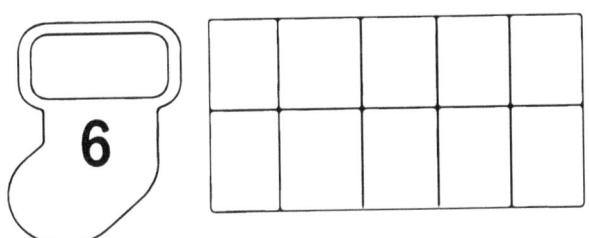
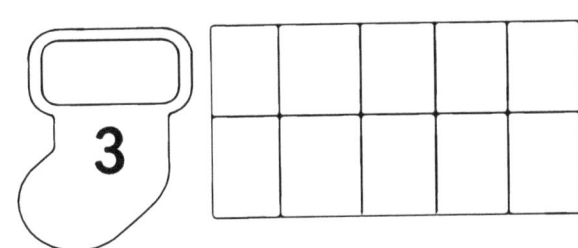
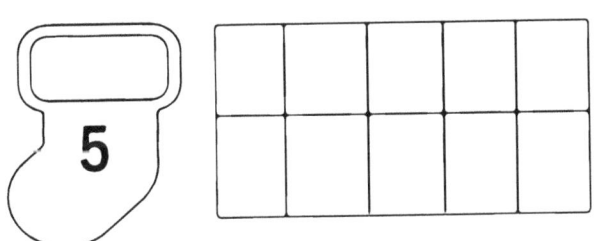
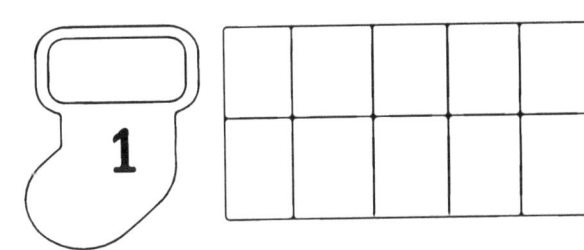
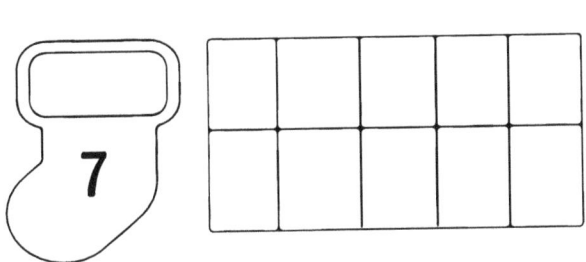
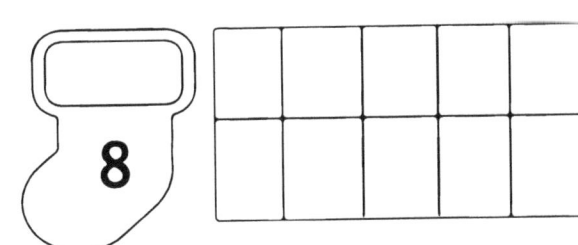

CHRISTMAS TEN FRAMES

NAME: _____

COLOR THE TEN FRAMES TO MATCH THE NUMBERS ON THE PIC

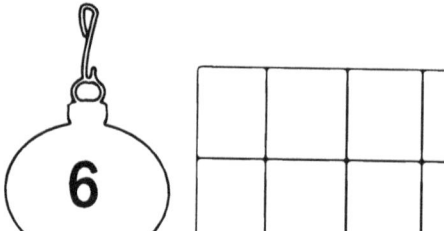  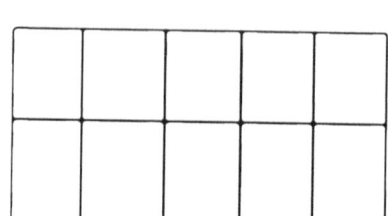

 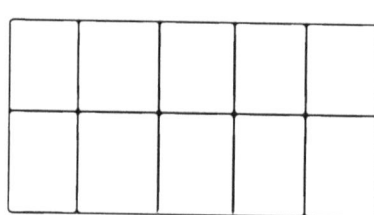  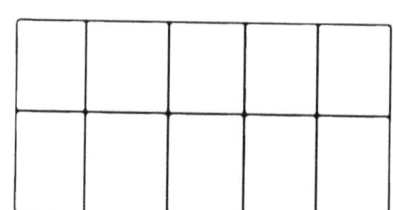

 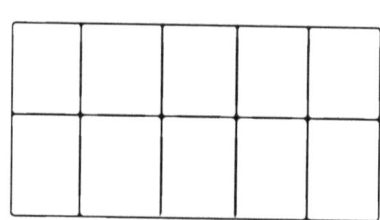  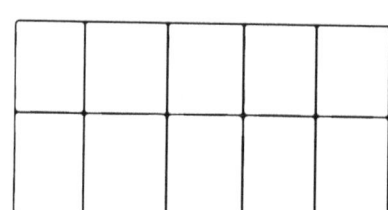

 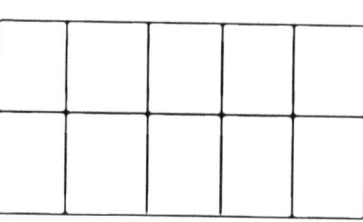  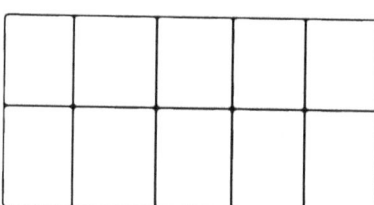

SNOWFLAKES TEN FRAMES

NAME: _____

COLOR THE TEN FRAMES TO MATCH THE NUMBERS ON THE PICTURE

- 2
- 5
- 4
- 1
- 7
- 9
- 8
- 10

CHRISTMAS TEN FRAMES

NAME: _____

COLOR THE TEN FRAMES TO MATCH THE NUMBERS ON THE PIC

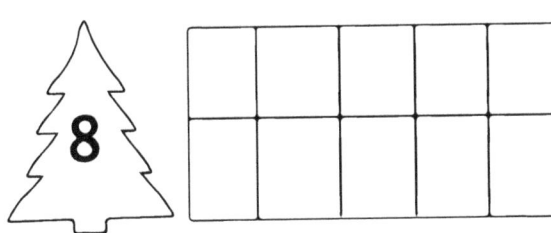
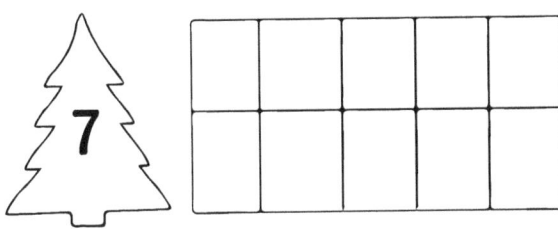
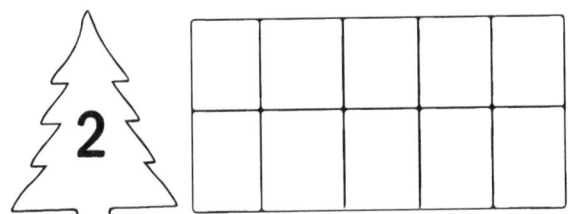
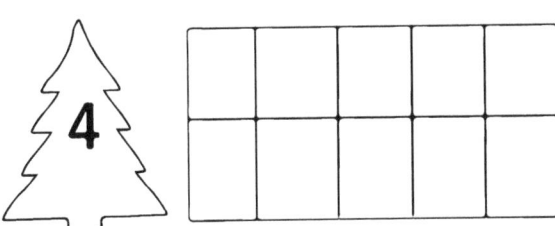
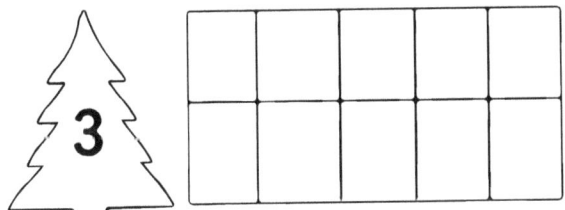
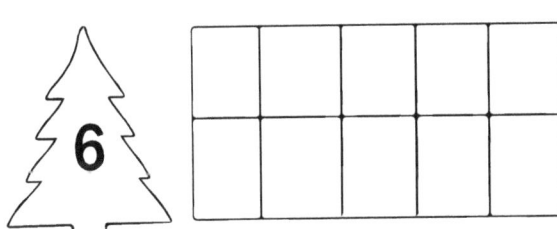
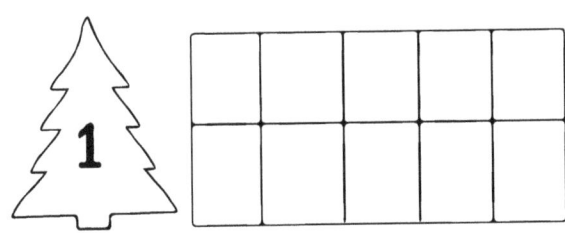
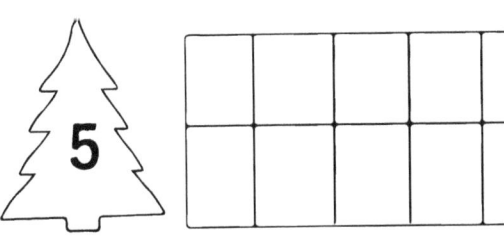

CHRISTMAS TEN FRAMES

NAME: _____

COLOR THE TEN FRAMES TO MATCH THE NUMBERS ON THE PIC

5		4	
9		2	
1		7	
 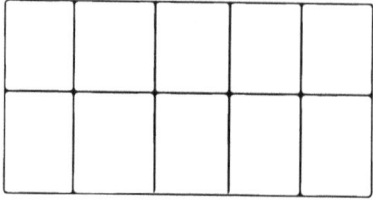  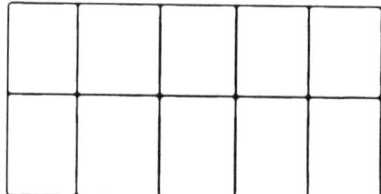

CHRISTMAS TEN FRAMES

NAME: _____

COLOR THE TEN FRAMES TO MATCH THE NUMBERS ON THE PIC

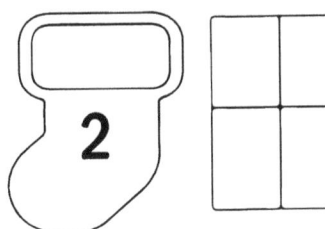 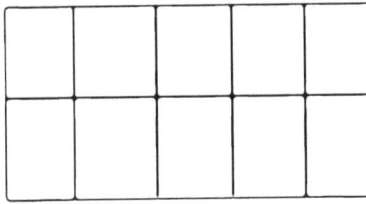 

 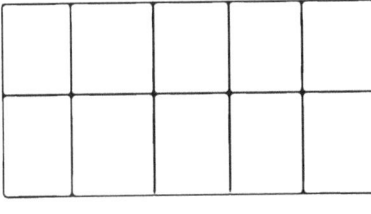

 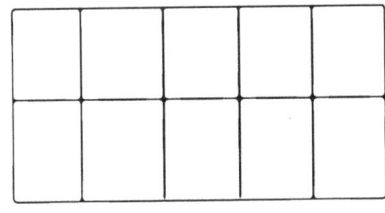 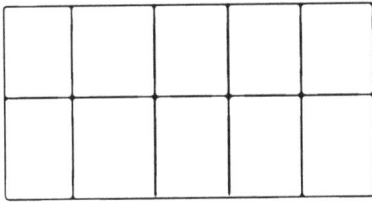

 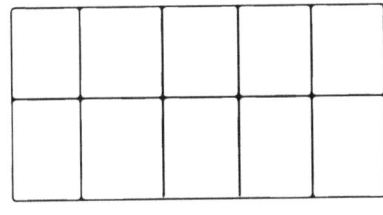

CHRISTMAS TEN FRAMES

NAME: _____

COLOR THE TEN FRAMES TO MATCH THE NUMBERS ON THE PIC

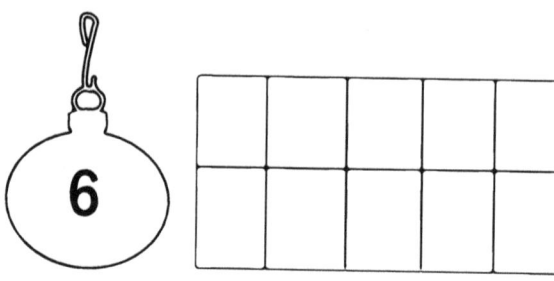

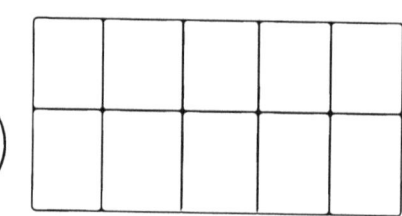

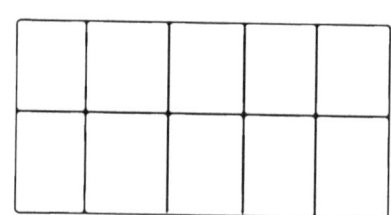

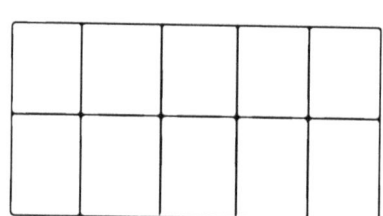

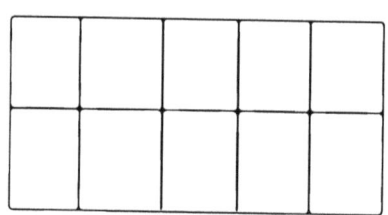

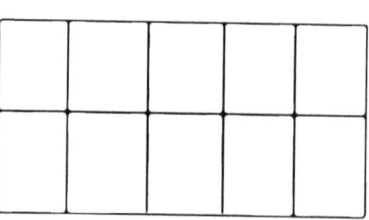

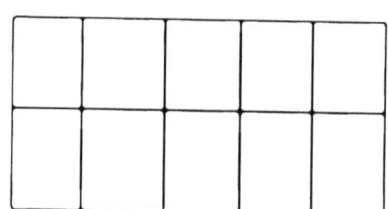

HELP THE ELF
FIND THE MISSING PRESENTS

MAZE SOLUTION

I SPY: CHRISTMAS

HOW MANY...

HELP THE ELF
FIND THE MISSING PRESENTS

MAZE SOLUTION

I SPY: CHRISTMAS

HOW MANY...

HELP THE ELF
FIND THE MISSING PRESENTS

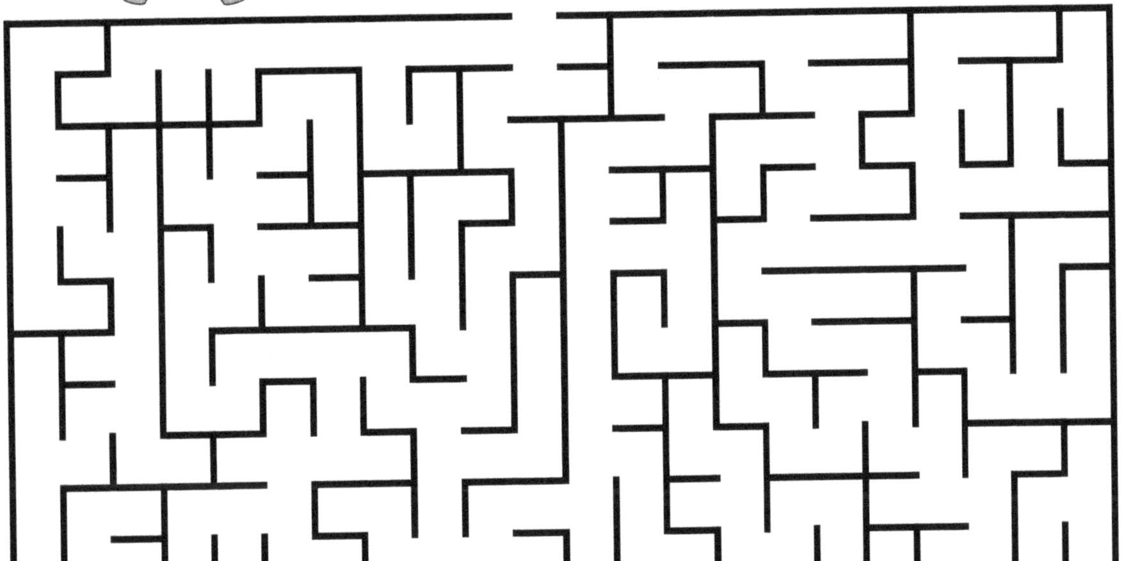

MAZE SOLUTION

I SPY: CHRISTMAS

HOW MANY...

 _____  _____  _____

 _____  _____  _____

HELP THE ELF
FIND THE MISSING PRESENTS

MAZE SOLUTION

I SPY: CHRISTMAS

HOW MANY...

HELP THE ELF
FIND THE MISSING PRESENTS

MAZE SOLUTION

I SPY: CHRISTMAS

HOW MANY...

HELP THE ELF
FIND THE MISSING PRESENTS

MAZE SOLUTION

I SPY: CHRISTMAS

HOW MANY...

Lightning Source UK Ltd.
Milton Keynes UK
UKHW030630160720
366640UK00009B/1031